To the drivers, past and present—MR

To my family—DK

Phaidon Press Limited
2 Cooperage Yard
London E15 2QR

Phaidon Press Inc.
111 Broadway
New York, NY 10006

Phaidon SARL
55, rue Traversière
75012 Paris

phaidon.com

First published 2026

Artwork created digitally

ISBN 978 1 83729 124 3 (US edition)
002-1125

A CIP catalog record for this book is available from the Library of Congress.

Printed in China

Commissioning Editor: Alice-May Bermingham
Project Editor: Rachel Craig-McFeely
Editorial Assistant: Nina Santoro
Production Controller: Rebecca Price
Design: Laura Hambleton

FORMULA FAST

YOUR ULTIMATE GUIDE TO FORMULA ONE RACING!

MATT RALPHS Illustrated by DRAGAN KORDIĆ

CONTENTS

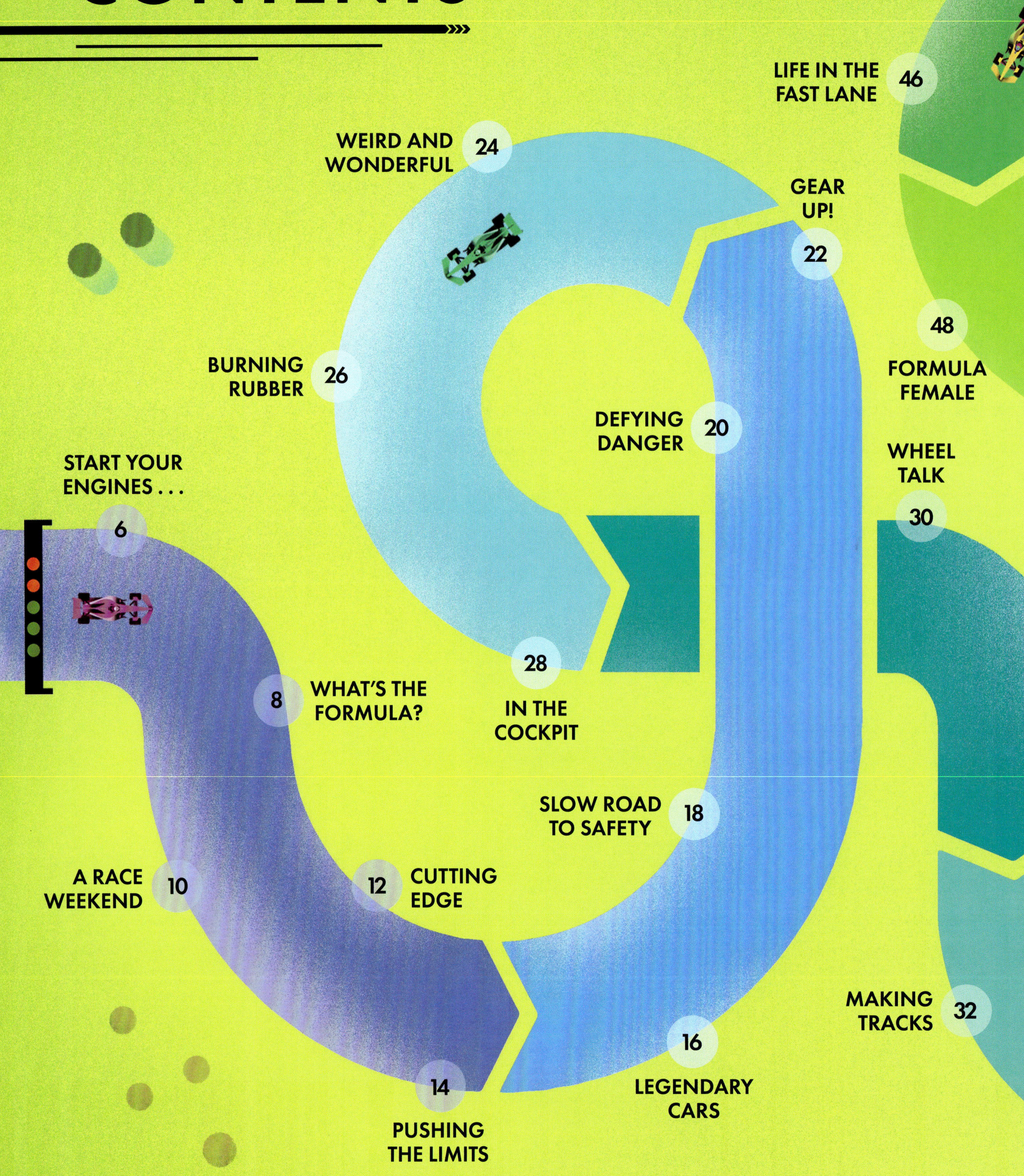

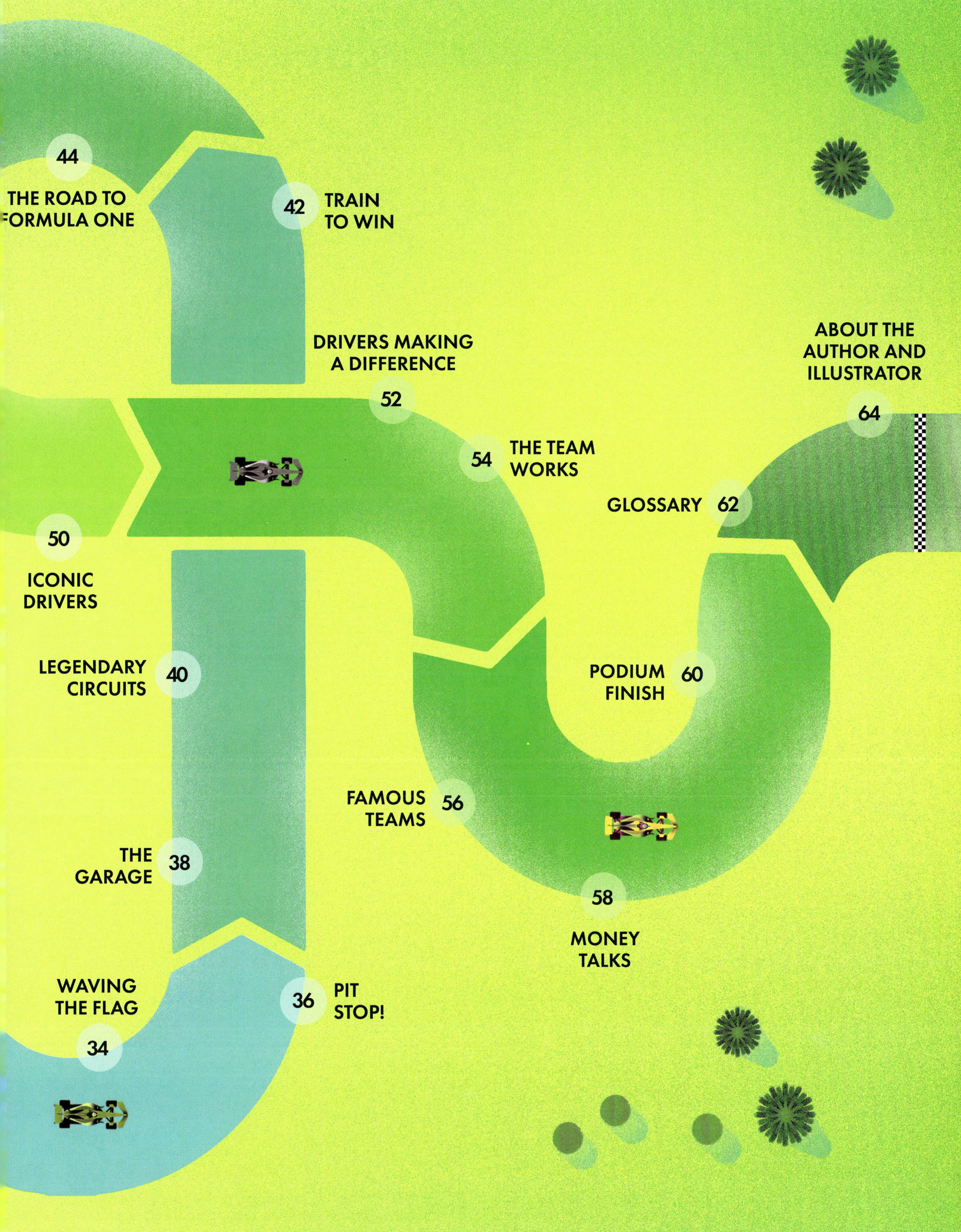

START YOUR ENGINES . . .

Have you ever watched a Formula One race?

Twenty-two sleek and shiny cars roll onto the racetrack. With their fat tires, bright colors and smooth lines, they look mean, built for speed . . . and built to win.

Inside the cars, each driver is focused and ready. Years of training have prepared them for this moment. The roar of engines fills the air. The drivers stare dead ahead, hands tight on the wheel. Their hearts beat faster. One by one, five pairs of red lights blink on . . .

There is simply nothing like a Formula One race. The world's best drivers zooming across tarmac. Multimillion-dollar, cutting-edge cars. A chance at fame, glory, and a place in motorsport history.

Sound like fun?

Buckle up and get ready to race!

WHAT'S THE FORMULA?

FORMULA ONE

"Formula" refers to the rules.

"One" means they're the best!

It is also known as "F1."

WHEN DO THEY RACE?

The Formula One season runs from March to December. There are 22–24 races. Each race is called a **Grand Prix**, French for "Big Prize."

Most Grand Prix are at least 190 miles long—that's almost as far as from New York City to Baltimore! The race involves driving **laps** around a track called a circuit.

WHO COMPETES?

Eleven racing teams compete in Formula One. The teams are known as "**constructors**." You've probably heard of some of them, like Ferrari or Mercedes. The eleventh team, Cadillac, only joined in 2026.

Every team must enter two cars per Grand Prix. Teams design and build their own cars in their own factories.

ARE THERE RULES?

There are lots! The Fédération Internationale de l'Automobile (**FIA**) sets the rules. These cover everything from car design, engine size, race format, and track to vehicle safety.

Breaking these rules leads to big penalties, including fines and losing points. A driver was once disqualified because one of his tires was too hot!

Formula One is the world's top motorsport. It's where the best drivers race the best cars on tracks all over the world. This super-speedy sport makes billions of dollars, inspires huge advances in technology, and provides excitement for its millions of global fans.

But what does Formula One actually involve?

HOW DO THEY WIN?

Twenty-two drivers compete in every Grand Prix. The drivers who finish in the top ten earn points. The driver and team with the most points at the end of the season win.

Each driver competes to win the **Drivers' Championship**. They also win points for their team to compete for the **Constructors' Championship**.

WHAT DOES *THAT* MEAN?

Formula One uses a LOT of technical words! To help you out, images will show you how some of these words are used.

Words or phrases in **bold** are explained more fully in the glossary on page 62.

Now you know the basics of Formula One.

Drive on to find out what happens on an actual race weekend!

A RACE WEEKEND

Every team and driver have one aim: to have a successful (and safe) Grand Prix race weekend. The schedule is jam-packed. Engineers, mechanics, and drivers must work nonstop before the race even begins . . .

PRACTICE

There are three one-hour-long practice sessions—two on Friday and one on Saturday. These are called Free Practice (FP).

Practice allows the team to gather **data**, test their car's performance, and make any last-minute changes. It also gives the driver precious time to get to know the track.

QUALIFYING

On Saturday there are three **Qualifying** stages: Q1, Q2, and Q3. The results decide the order the drivers start on race day (their **grid position**).

The drivers race as fast as they can around the track. In Q1 and Q2, the slowest twelve drivers are removed. They will start in positions 11–22 on race day. Q3 decides the order the top ten drivers start in.

SPRINT IT TO WIN IT

Some race weekends have an exciting extra element: sprint races. The drivers compete in a 62-mile dash to the finish line—there's no time to stop!

Championship points up are for grabs, so these sprints work like mini Grand Prix.

RACE DAY

Sunday is race day. After warm-up laps, the drivers perform a slow lap to heat up their tires. Then they line up in order. The crowd goes quiet. One by one, five pairs of starting lights come on. When the lights go out, the race begins!

The drivers zoom around the circuit. At intervals throughout the race, they pause briefly for **pit stops**. The first car to cross the finish line wins.

CUTTING EDGE

A world-class driver needs a cutting-edge car. The modern Formula One car is the coolest, most high-tech car on the planet.

What are the features that make it so incredible?

REAR WING

The rear wing's unique shape creates **downforce**, or pressure that helps the car "stick" to the track. This helps the car's **cornering** (making turns on the track) and **handling** (control) at high speeds.

POWER UNIT

This powers the car. Formula One cars use "hybrid" power units, which use fuel and electricity. They combine a gas engine—a V6 **internal combustion engine (ICE)**—with an **Energy Recovery System (ERS)**, which stores extra energy for speed boosts.

GEARBOX

Sometimes called the "transmission," the gearbox connects the engine to the driving wheels. It helps the car go faster or slower by changing how the engine's power is used, like how changing gears on a bike makes pedaling easier or harder.

FUEL CELL

Also called a fuel tank, the fuel cell is like an unpuncturable balloon filled with gas. You are allowed to use up to 242 pounds (lb) of fuel per race—that's about the same weight as a newborn elephant!

The average max speed for a modern Formula One car is around 210–220 miles per hour (mph). That's about as quick as the fastest animal on Earth: the peregrine falcon (when it's diving for prey!) In fact, the trophy presented at the Abu Dhabi Grand Prix looks like a peregrine falcon.

AIRBOX

The power unit needs oxygen to burn gas, which creates energy to move the car. As the car moves forward, air flows into the airbox and down into the engine, mixing oxygen with the fuel.

CHASSIS

The **chassis** is the "load-bearing" part of the car. Its strong and stable frame attaches to, or links, all of the car's other parts. Formula One cars have a "**monocoque**" chassis, meaning the car's outer shell holds its main weight.

FRONT WING

Like the rear wing, the front wing helps to "stick" the car to the track. It can also be adjusted for each track: tracks with many straight sections require more speed and less **grip**; tracks with many tight corners require less speed and more grip.

SUSPENSION SYSTEM

The suspension system connects the wheels to the chassis. It helps the car stay stable when cornering at high speeds, and absorbs the impact from bumps and collisions.

WHEELS

Formula One cars have four wheels, made up of rubber tires attached to wheel discs (the part inside the tire). The wheel discs are made from a strong, lightweight metal called magnesium.

PUSHING THE LIMITS

Formula One cars weren't so high-tech to begin with. Since the first World Championship Grand Prix in 1950, engineers have pushed the limits of technology to build today's super-fast cars. Here's how they've changed over time.

Which of these cars would you want to drive?

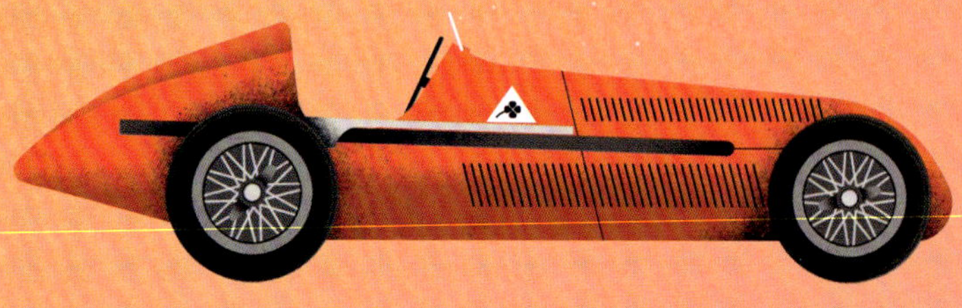

1950

The first Formula One cars were ordinary cars with alterations. They had open **cockpits** (where the driver sits), thin wheels, and a front-mounted engine, like this **ALFA ROMEO 158**.

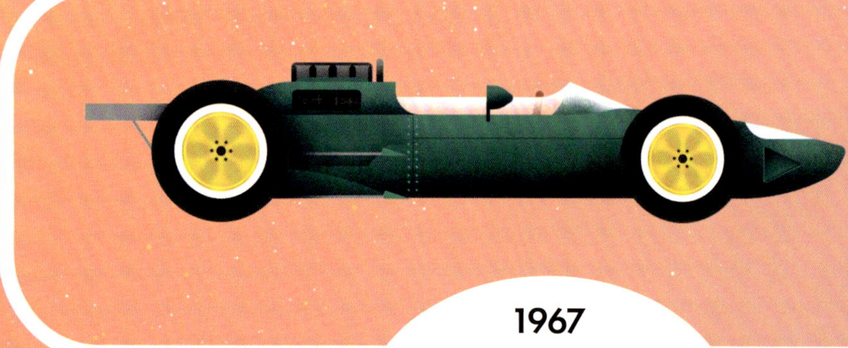

1967

The **LOTUS 49** used a "stressed member engine." The engine is part of the frame, and helps carry the weight of the car. This makes the body more compact and stronger.

The **MCLAREN MP4/1** had a chassis made entirely from a light but strong material called carbon fiber. Most cars are now made from this.

1981–83

Over time, electronically controlled parts were added to the cars. This **WILLIAMS FW15C** had high-tech features such as **active suspension**, **anti-lock brakes**, and **traction control**.

1993

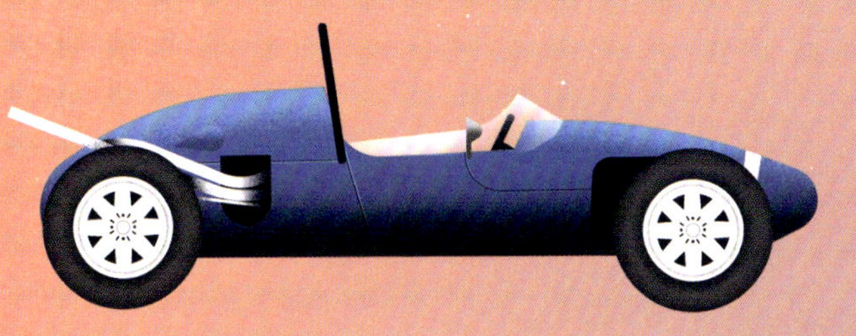

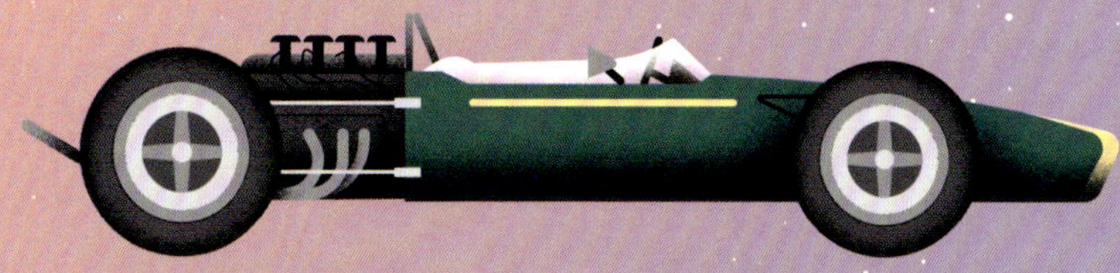

1958

Moving the engine behind the driver made the car more balanced and easier to control. The first "mid-engine" design to win a Grand Prix was this **COOPER T43**.

1962

The **LOTUS 25** was the first car to have a monocoque chassis. This revolutionary design increased the car's strength. It's been used by all Formula One teams ever since!

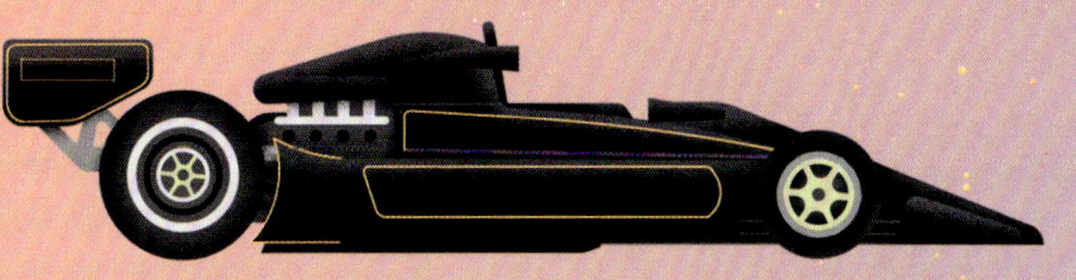

1977–78

The **LOTUS 78** was the first "**ground effect**" car. This means its shape helps the car "stick" to the ground with downforce, making the car more stable when turning. Rival teams scrambled to copy this effect.

1977–78

The first Formula One car sporting a **turbocharged engine** was the **RENAULT RS01**. A turbocharger pulls more air into the engine, making it even more powerful! All Formula One cars are now turbocharged.

All Formula One cars (such as this **MERCEDES F1 W05**) now have hybrid power units. These still allow cars to go fast, but are much more fuel efficient. This is part of F1's mission to become more environmentally friendly.

2014–NOW

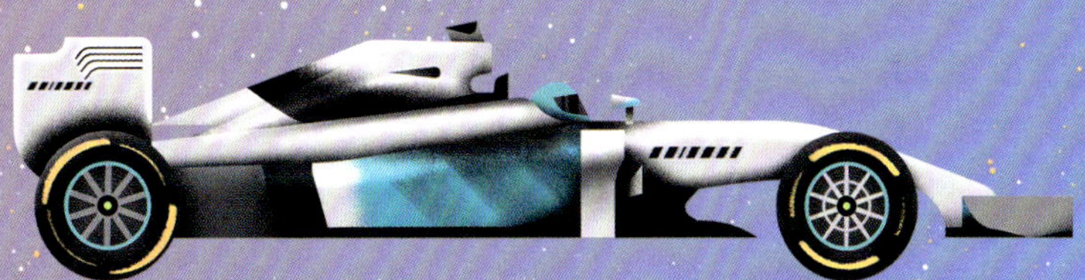

LEGENDARY CARS

A lot of cars have raced over Formula One's long history. Most have small (but important) improvements. But some break the mold to create pure racing magic. These become true mechanical legends.

FERRARI 500

This red beauty won the very first race it entered (the 1952 Swiss Grand Prix) and dominated for two years. It had a front-mounted engine and a four-speed **manual gearbox**, where the driver presses a pedal called the **clutch** and moves a "stick" to change gears.

MERCEDES W196

This silver bullet streaked ahead of the pack. It had an engine developed using fighter plane technology! Driven by legends such as Juan Manuel Fangio and Stirling Moss, it won two Drivers' Championships in 1954 and 1955.

MCLAREN-HONDA MP4/4

Built around a Honda 1.5 liter V6 turbocharged engine, this is one of the most successful Formula One cars. In the expert hands of teammates (and rivals) Alain Prost and Ayrton Senna, it won an amazing fifteen of its sixteen races in the 1988 Championship.

WILLIAMS FW14B

With a **semiautomatic gearbox**, traction control, and active suspension, this car was miles ahead of its rivals. Driven by British racer Nigel Mansell, it won both the Drivers' and Constructors' Championships in 1992.

FERRARI F2002

Another red wonder with a powerful engine (a monstrous 3-liter V10), this Ferrari was driven to win after win by German Michael Schumacher in the 2002 season. After winning both the Constructors' and Drivers' Championships, it was even used to kick off the 2003 season.

MERCEDES W05 HYBRID

When gas engines were replaced with hybrid power units in 2014, Mercedes rose to the challenge with their 1.6 liter V6 turbocharged PU106A engine. This car won that year's Constructors' and the Drivers' Championship for Lewis Hamilton.

RED BULL RB19

Crushing the competition in the 2023 season, this car—driven by aces Sergio Pérez and Max Verstappen—won twenty-one of the twenty-two races. It claimed both the Drivers' (for Verstappen) and Constructors' Championships.

SLOW ROAD TO SAFETY

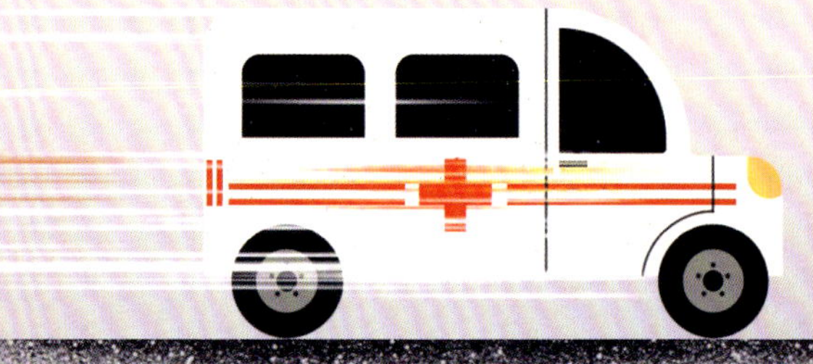

1950s

1950–60s

THE EARLY DAYS

In the 1950s, most of the driver's head and shoulders were completely unprotected. Drivers didn't even have to wear a helmet until 1952, and they were mostly made of cork.

There were no seat belts either—the argument went that in an accident, it was better to be thrown clear of the car than to be trapped inside.

SPECTATOR SAFETY

In the early days, people were allowed to stand unprotected right next to the track. "Safety" barriers were nothing more than piles of hay bales, which could easily catch fire.

Formula One fans want to be thrilled by exciting wheel-to-wheel racing, but without anyone getting hurt. Crashes do happen, but thankfully the high-tech safety gear means modern-day drivers usually walk away unharmed. But that wasn't always the case . . .

1961

1966

AWFUL ACCIDENTS

One of the very worst Formula One crashes occurred at Monza in 1961. Wolfgang von Trips's Ferrari collided with Jim Clark's Lotus, lost control, and spun straight into the crowd. Fifteen spectators and von Trips were killed. Shockingly, the race continued—today, it would have been stopped.

EMERGENCY SERVICES

During the 1966 Spa-Francorchamps Grand Prix, Jackie Stewart crashed his BRM P261 into a telegraph pole. He was trapped in the wreckage for twenty-five minutes. He was eventually rescued by other drivers who had crashed in the same spot.

Crashes like this led drivers to argue for better safety. Today, drivers can expect emergency services to show up quickly.

DEFYING DANGER

Driving the world's best racing cars around twisting tracks with twenty-one other ultra-competitive drivers is dangerous. But Formula One's modern era is the safest ever. Advances in Formula One safety technology have even been used in ordinary cars—and made motorsport more accessible. It's a win-win!

HALO

Formula One cars have an open cockpit. This means if the car rolls over, the driver's head is at risk. From 2018, all Formula One cars were fitted with a Halo device: a **titanium** frame over the cockpit that protects the head if the car flips.

SURVIVAL CELL

The survival cell is like an armored cocoon, protecting the driver during crashes. While wings might crumple and wheels fly off, the survival cell absorbs impact but stays in one piece.

FIRE SUPPRESSION SYSTEM

Protecting the driver (and spectators) from fire is really important. All Formula One cars have a fire suppression system that sprays special foam into the engine and cockpit after an accident to stop fire from spreading.

HEADREST

Designed to protect the driver from impact, these U-shaped headrests are made with memory foam (a material that "remembers" the shape of the driver's head). They are shaped to fit the driver perfectly.

SAFETY HARNESS

Drivers are secured inside their cockpit with a six-strap safety harness to keep them inside the survival cell during a crash. A twist of the hand unfastens the harness for a quick escape.

DATA GATHERING

Formula One cars are covered in electronic sensors detecting things such as speed and **G-force** limits. Technicians analyze this data to help them understand the forces acting on the car, and how they can make the driver safer.

GEAR UP!

A driver's safety is the top priority. Teams spend huge amounts of time and money making the best wearable gear for their drivers to keep them safe and comfortable.

Would you wear this outfit?

UNDERWEAR

The first thing drivers put on is a set of **breathable**, fire-resistant, head-to-toe underwear. They wear a balaclava (a tight, stretchy covering over the scalp, ears, neck, and most of the face), pants, a long-sleeved top, and socks.

RACE SUIT

This one-piece suit covers everything except the head, hands, and feet. It protects the driver from fires up to 1,472°F for at least twelve seconds (enough time to exit a burning car). Drivers get very hot during a race. Their suit is lightweight and breathable to keep them cool.

HANS (HEAD AND NECK SUPPORT)

During a crash, the driver's head is often thrown forward while the upper body is kept still by the safety harness. The Head and Neck Support (HANS) prevents neck injuries by connecting the helmet to the seat belts.

HELMET

Drivers wear full-face helmets, which means when the visor is down, the head and face are completely covered. Helmets protect drivers from fire and impact in crashes. They are also decorated for each driver so fans can recognize them!

GLOVES

A driver's close-fitting, tailor-made gloves are not only fire resistant, they also read **biometric** information using built-in sensors. This information can be sent to emergency responders to help them check on a driver after an accident.

BOOTS

Drivers need to be able to feel the pedals with their feet. This is why drivers' boots are more like socks, with thin, flat rubber soles to "grip" the pedals.

WEIRD AND WONDERFUL

In the ultra-competitive world of Formula One, car designers have dreamed up truly radical ideas—some successful, some not—that make fans say, "Wow, that car is *weird*."

Which of these cars do you think is the weirdest?

FERGUSON P99

This was the only **four-wheel drive** car to ever win a Formula One race. Most cars have two wheels connected to the engine—in four-wheel drive cars, all four are!

LOTUS 56B

Formula One cars act like upside-down airplane wings, "sticking" the car to the track rather than lifting it into the air. This car went one step further by using an airplane engine. It never won a race.

ENSIGN N179

Ensign Racing was a 1970s British Formula One racing team. One of their cars, the Ensign N179, has been called the ugliest Formula One car ever built. It wasn't a success and didn't last long.

TYRRELL P34

Are six wheels better than four? Tyrrell Racing's six-wheeled wonder astonished the world. The P34 finished first and second in the 1976 Swedish Grand Prix.

BRABHAM BT46B

Known as the "fan car," the BT46B had a powerful fan fixed to its rear. This one-off won one Grand Prix in 1978. Because of complaints from the other teams, it was withdrawn.

Four-wheel drive cars are no longer allowed in Formula One—only the rear wheels are connected to the power unit.

The Pratt & Whitney ST6 **gas turbine** engine (used in aircraft, helicopters, and hovercraft) was lightweight and powerful, but guzzled fuel.

It was nicknamed the "cheese grater" because of the three large **radiators** that looked like steps up from the front wing.

Four of the six wheels were unusually small. This increased the car's grip, reduced **drag** (a force that slows the car down), and improved braking.

The designers claimed that the fan was to cool down the engine. But the fan also sucked air out from under the car, greatly improving grip and cornering.

BURNING RUBBER

Tires are a major part of any team's racing strategy. After all, they're the only part of the car that actually touches the track! Different types of tires, called "compounds," are color-coded to help fans spot which tires their favorite drivers are using.

TIRE RULES

There are limits on the number of tire sets (one set = four tires) teams can use over a race weekend. For a standard weekend, each driver has thirteen sets of slicks (eight softs, three mediums, two hards) and seven grooved (four intermediates and three wets).

Teams can change their tires as many times as they want during a race—but each change (called a "pit stop") takes time. Most races involve two pit stops.

Soft, medium, and hard compounds are called "slicks" because their surface is smooth. This helps the tire grip the track.

SOFTS

Red tires are made from the softest rubber. This gives the best grip, so the driver can turn corners faster—but they wear out quickly.

MEDIUMS

Yellow medium tires sit between softs and hards. They have more grip than hards, but don't last as long. They have less grip than softs but last longer.

HARDS

White hard tires last the longest before needing to be replaced, but they lack the grip—and so the control—of softs and mediums.

INTERMEDIATES

Green intermediate tires are used in wet weather. They have grooves to remove water from the track and improve grip.

WETS

Blue wet tires are used in very wet weather. Grooves remove water from under the wheel to reduce the chance of hydroplaning (sliding uncontrollably on a wet track).

IN THE COCKPIT

To compete, driver and car must be in perfect tune, working together to cross the finish line in the fastest time, and as safely as possible. An ordinary driver's license won't do, either. You'll need an FIA Super Licence to compete!

SEAT

No two Formula One driver seats are the same: each is molded to fit its driver. Unlike an ordinary car, the driver sits in a reclined position—almost lying down—with their feet raised to use the pedals.

Much like you would on a roller coaster, drivers experience G-forces up to five times their own body weight! The seat helps the driver stay comfortable and fairly still, despite these forces.

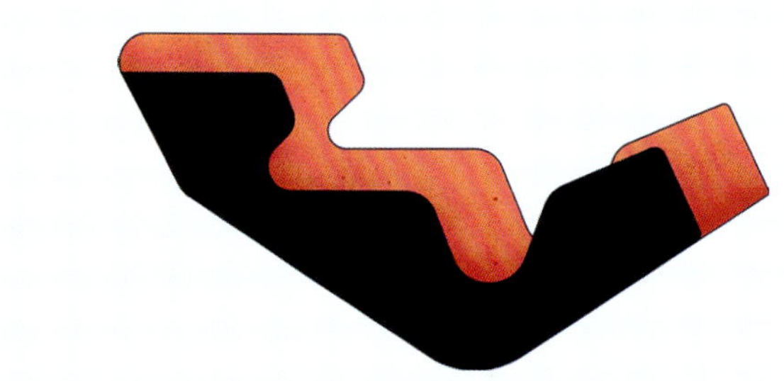

PEDALS

Formula One cars have two pedals. On the right is the accelerator (to speed up); on the left is the brake (to slow down).

Pedal positions can be adjusted to suit the driver. The surface of each pedal is roughly textured for maximum grip against the shoe, with a raised frame to stop the driver's feet from sliding off.

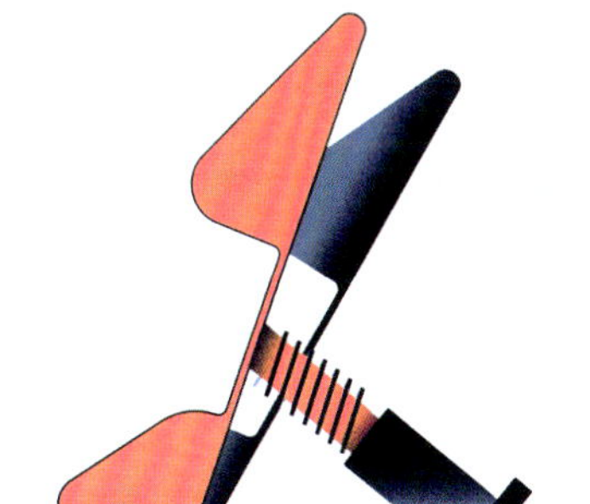

COCKPIT

This armored shell contains the driver and their car controls. The driver's view from the cockpit is limited, with sides so high they can't see their own front wing, or rival cars to the side or slightly behind. They can't even see the edge of the track as they turn!

WHEEL TALK

Formula One steering wheels look more like game controllers than ordinary steering wheels! The wheel is customized to each driver. Dozens of buttons, paddles, and switches can be programmed to do hundreds of jobs.

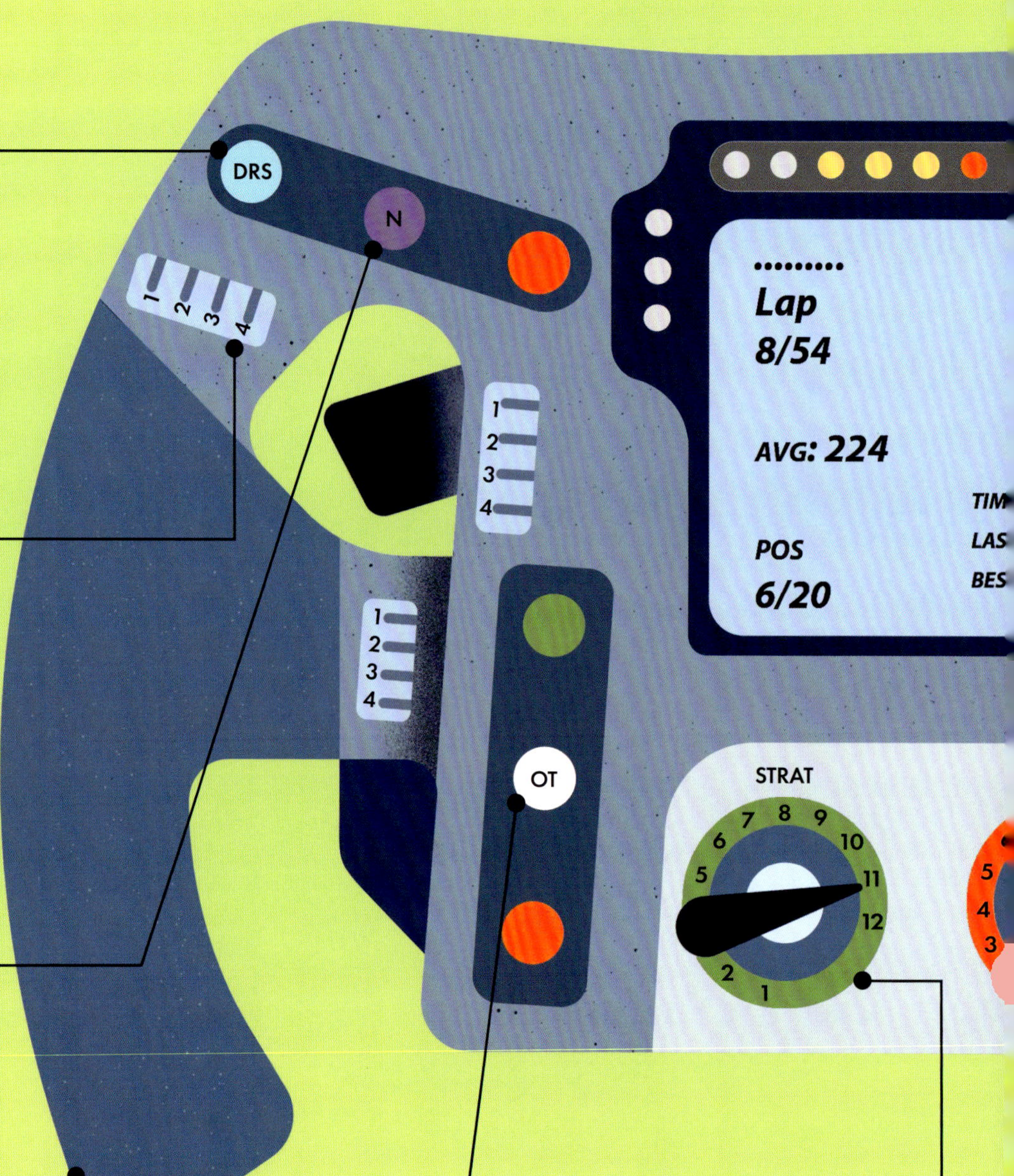

DRAG REDUCTION SYSTEM (DRS)

Pressing this opens the car's rear wing. This reduces drag and provides an extra burst of speed.

DIFFERENTIAL

This switch changes the balance between the back wheels. Correctly adjusting it when cornering means the car only loses a little speed, while keeping grip.

NEUTRAL

This puts the car into neutral (a gear that disconnects the engine from the driving wheels). It is only pressed when the car has stopped.

GRIPS

Grips (or handles) are made from rubber using a mold of the driver's hands. All the wheel's buttons are within reach of their thumbs.

OVERTAKE

This button releases stored battery energy to give the car a speed boost. It is usually used when drivers are trying to **overtake** (go past another car).

STRAT

"Strat" stands for "strategy." This switch changes the engine mode, usually to alter its power. For example, it can be adjusted to give the engine extra power to overtake.

DISPLAY SCREEN

This provides vital information, such as the car's speed, gear, and lap numbers.

LEDS

Light-emitting diodes (LEDs) show the driver key information. Some flash in different colors to show the track's condition.

PIT LIMITER

This prevents the car from going faster than the speed limit (usually 50 mph) in the pit lane (see page 33).

PIT CONFIRM

Drivers press this to confirm they are coming in for a pit stop. It warns the pit crew to get ready.

GEAR PADDLES

Gear changes—called upshifts and downshifts—are made using these finger-paddles on either side of the wheel.

TALK

In a race, driver and team are in constant communication. This button opens and closes a radio channel between them, similar to a walkie-talkie.

HPP

This adjusts the power unit settings for the hybrid engine. These are usually set by engineers before the race begins.

BBaL

Pressing this changes the brake balance between the front and rear wheels. This affects the car's stability: too much rear brake can cause the car to spin; too much front brake can stop it from turning.

CLUTCH

Used to start and stop the car. The driver holds one of the clutch paddles at the start of the race, and releases it when the starting lights go out to begin racing.

MAKING TRACKS

Just as each Formula One car is unique, so, too, are the tracks. There are Grand Prix tracks all over the world. Most are specially built; some use closed-off public roads. They can be long or short, fast or (relatively) slow. But every track has these elements.

1. STARTING GRID
Where the action begins. The drivers line up for the race start in the order of their Qualifying times. The finish line is usually here as well.

2. STARTING LIGHTS
Five sets of two lights turn red, one after the other. The race begins when the lights go out!

3. HAIRPIN BENDS
Very tight corners where drivers need to reduce their speed. They usually involve turning the car around in a half-circle.

4. STRAIGHTS
Time to put your foot down! Long and straight, these are the fastest sections of track with average top speeds of around 215 mph.

5. SECTORS
Formula One tracks are split into three roughly equal "sectors." Drivers are timed in each sector to give teams information about how they compare to their rivals.

6. DRS DETECTION ZONES

Section of a track—usually a straight—where drivers are allowed to activate their Drag Reduction System.

7. CORNERS

On corners, drivers try to find the best "racing line." That means passing through in as straight a line as possible so they can exit the corner at maximum speed.

8. CHICANES

A tricky series of bends, one right after the other. These force cars to slow down, often before a long, fast straight.

9. GRANDSTANDS

Huge tiered seating areas for fans, placed around different parts of the track. There is always one alongside the starting grid. Which grandstand would you watch from?

10. PODIUM

A platform where, after the race, the top three drivers get their trophies and spray each other (and the crowd!) with Champagne.

11. PIT LANE

A stretch of track alongside the starting grid. All the team garages are here. Cars enter when they need repairs or a tire change. The area outside the garage where the pit stop happens is called the pit box.

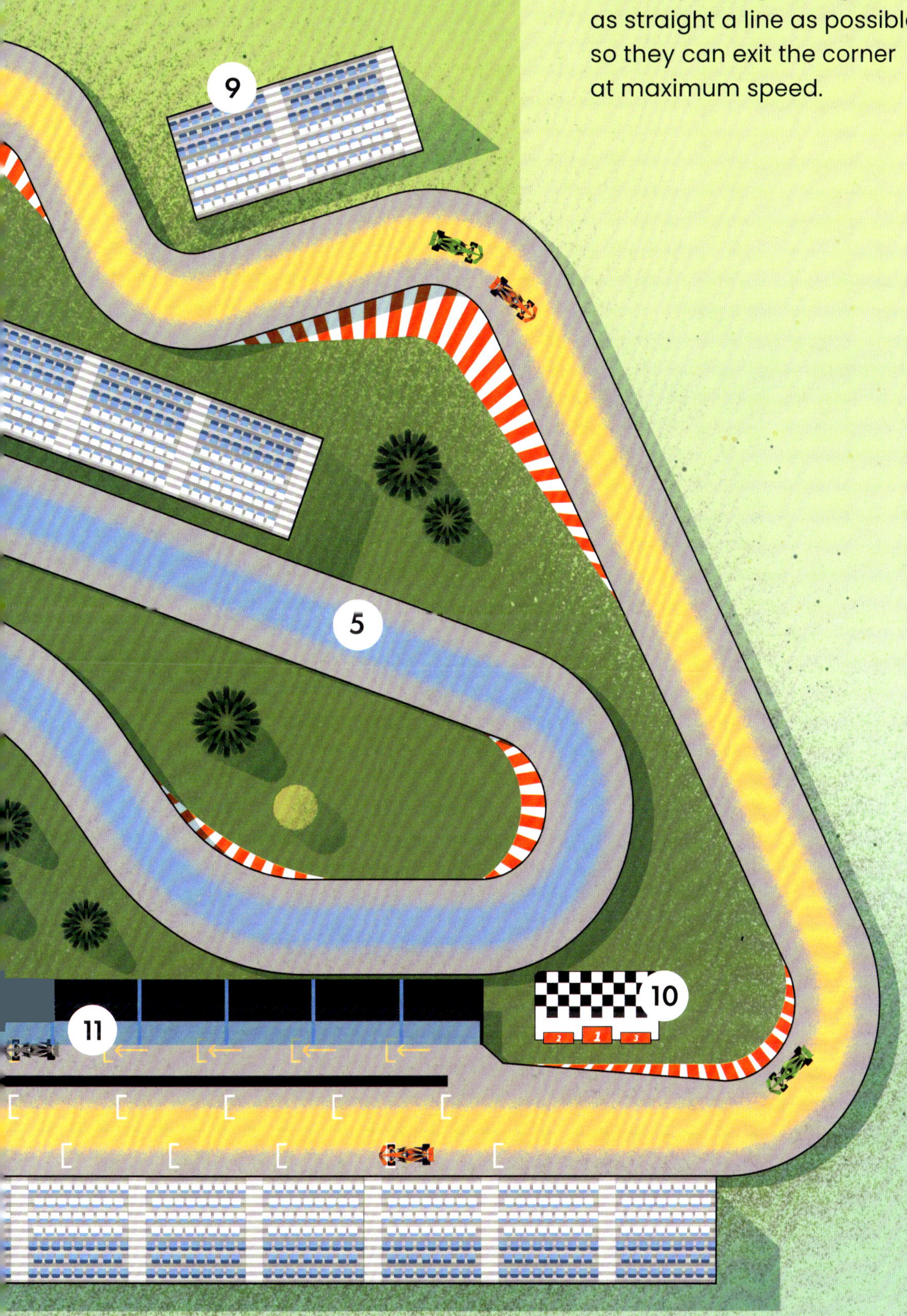

There are between 48 and 78 laps in each Grand Prix! That means a race typically takes about 90 minutes.

WAVING THE FLAG

As high-tech as modern Grand Prix circuits may be, nothing beats an old-fashioned flag to give drivers information.

Do you know what these flags mean?

GREEN

This tells drivers that all hazards have been cleared and they are free to race at top speed and overtake.

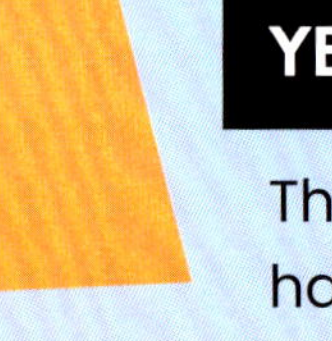

YELLOW

This means there are hazards ahead. A single yellow means slow down and prepare to change direction; double yellow means slow down and prepare to stop. No overtaking is allowed.

RED

This means the race has been suspended, usually due to a serious accident or very severe weather. All drivers must return to the pit lane.

WHITE

This warns drivers that slow-moving vehicles—such as ambulances, tow trucks, or broken-down cars—are on the track. They need to slow down and be careful.

BLACK

This means that a driver has been disqualified. This flag is serious and rare, but is sometimes given for dangerous driving or if the car is not following technical rules.

BLUE

This flag is waved at a driver about to be **lapped**. The slower driver must let the faster car overtake—or they'll get a penalty.

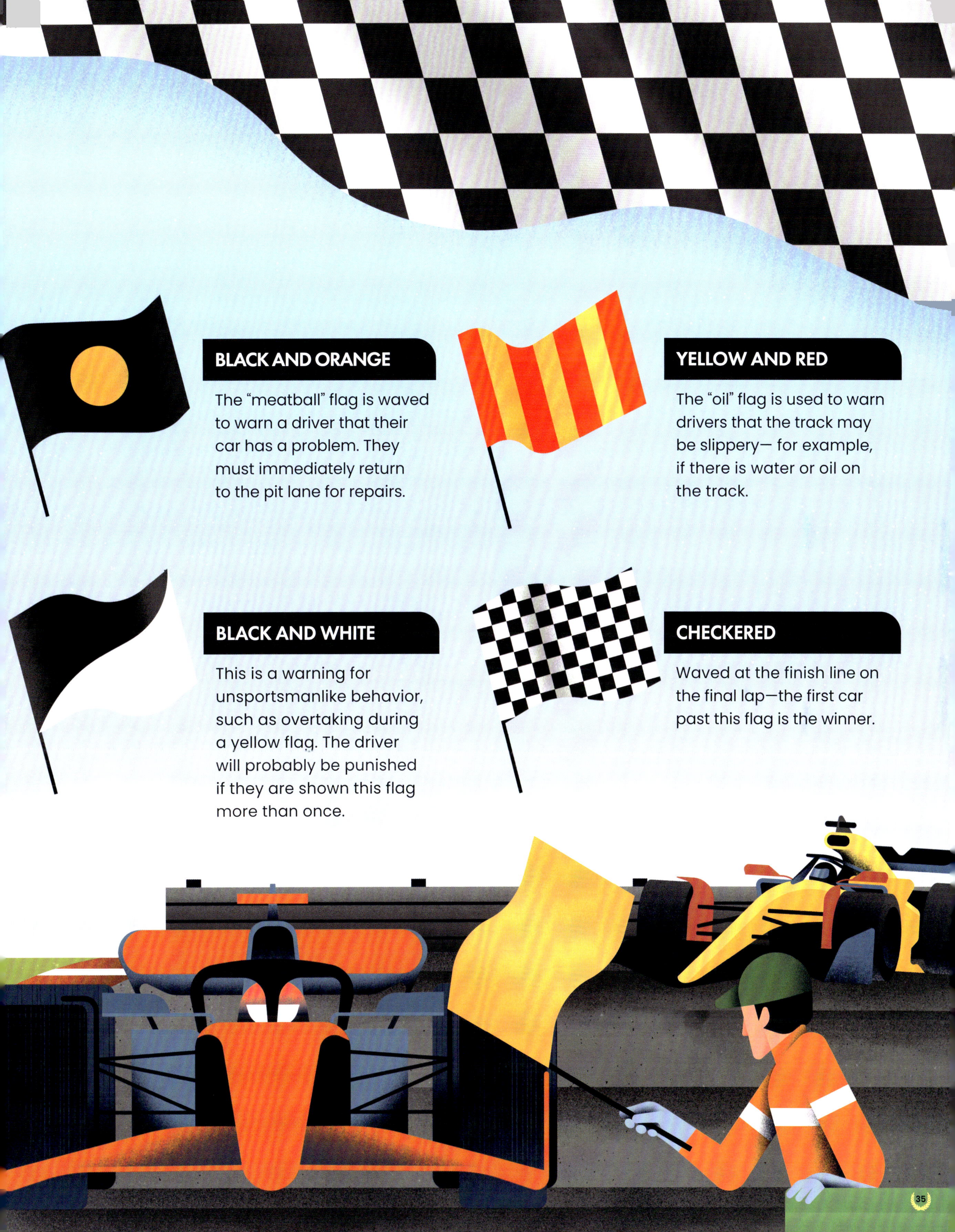

BLACK AND ORANGE

The "meatball" flag is waved to warn a driver that their car has a problem. They must immediately return to the pit lane for repairs.

YELLOW AND RED

The "oil" flag is used to warn drivers that the track may be slippery— for example, if there is water or oil on the track.

BLACK AND WHITE

This is a warning for unsportsmanlike behavior, such as overtaking during a yellow flag. The driver will probably be punished if they are shown this flag more than once.

CHECKERED

Waved at the finish line on the final lap—the first car past this flag is the winner.

PIT STOP!

When a driver hears the words "Box! Box!" over their radio, they get ready for one of the most intense parts of the race: the pit stop. This is when the car stops in the pit lane for tire changes and repairs. A pit stop longer than 2.5 seconds is slow!

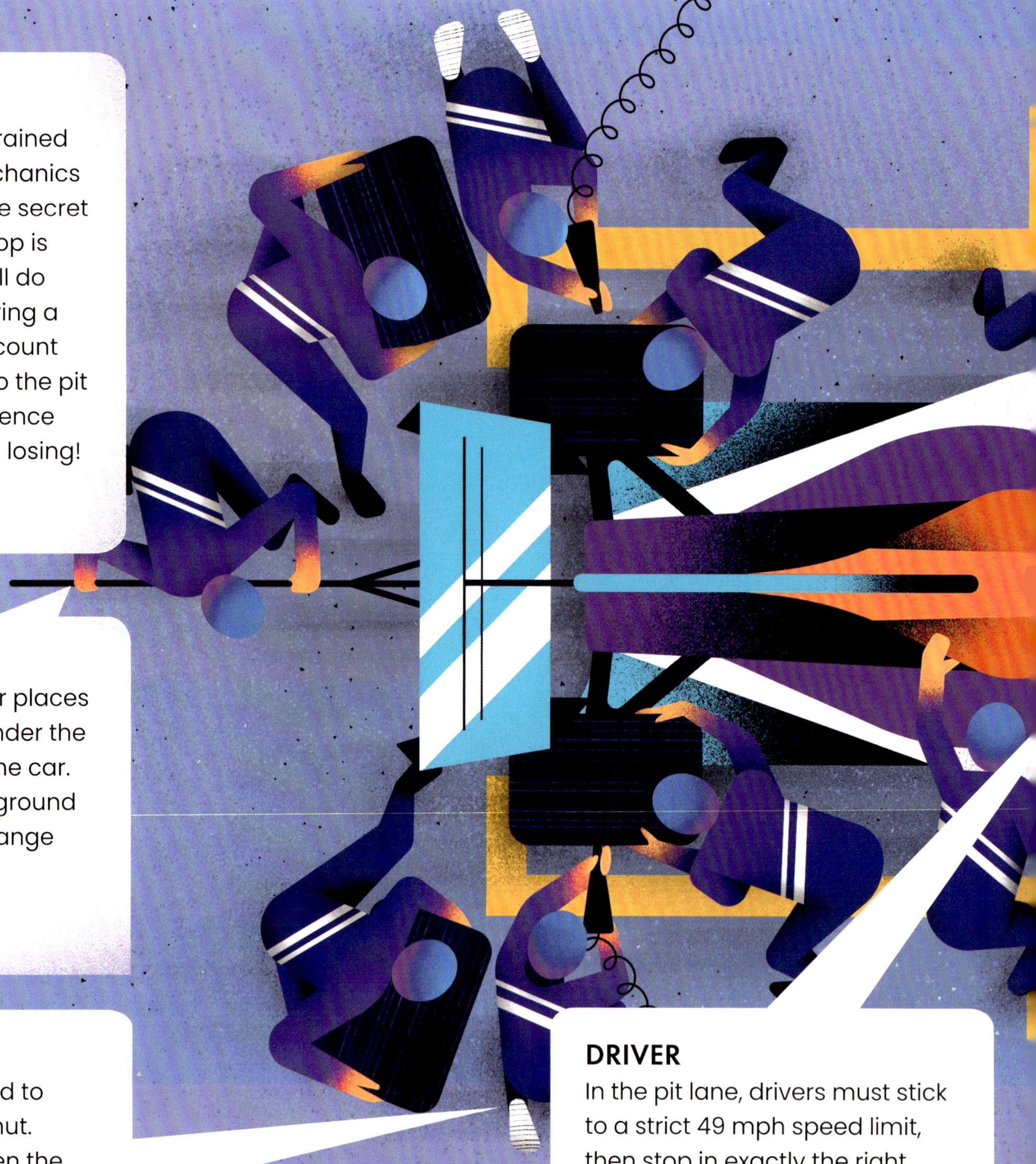

PIT CREW

About twenty highly trained and physically fit mechanics make up the crew. The secret recipe for a fast pit stop is practice—the crew will do around 1,000 drills during a season. Milliseconds count during a Grand Prix, so the pit stop can be the difference between winning and losing!

REAR JACK

The rear jack operator places a tool called a jack under the **indicator light** to lift the car. Lifting the car off the ground allows the crew to change the tires.

TIRE GUNNER

Each wheel is fastened to the car with a wheel nut. The tire gunners loosen the wheel nut (to remove the old tire), then tighten it again (to put on the new one).

DRIVER

In the pit lane, drivers must stick to a strict 49 mph speed limit, then stop in exactly the right place in the pit box. Get it wrong, and the pit crew will need to move, wasting precious time.

STEADIERS

At least two steadiers hold the car to keep it still while it's up on jacks. If there's time, they also wipe down the mirrors and driver's visor.

TIRE OFF

The tire-off operator lugs the old tire from the car as soon as the nut has been loosened.

THE OVERSEER

This is usually the chief mechanic, who also oversees the pit stop. They only release the driver when all work is complete and the pit lane is clear.

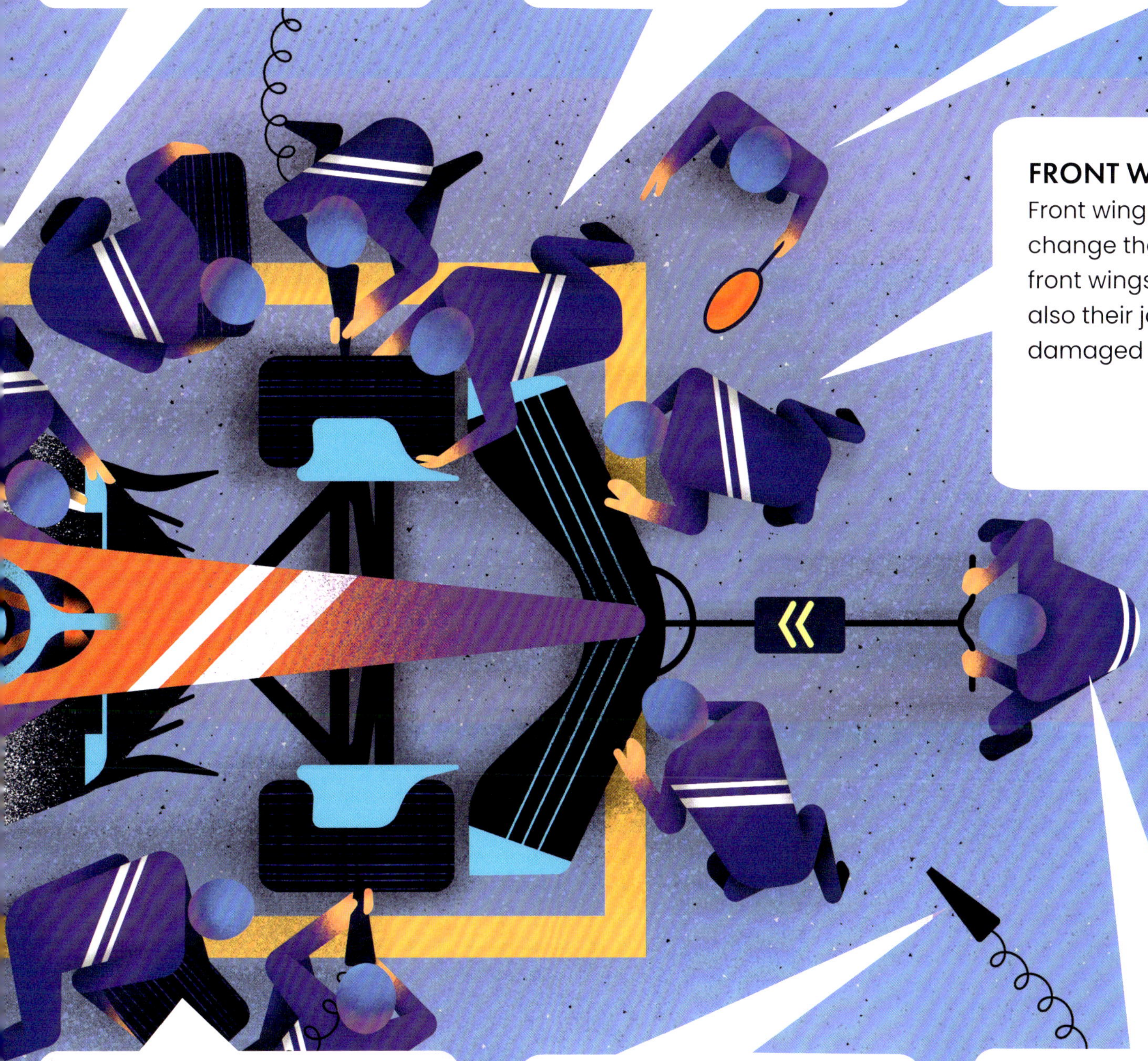

FRONT WING ADJUST

Front wing adjusters change the angle of the front wings, if needed. It's also their job to replace damaged front wings.

TIRE ON

The moment the old tire is removed, the tire-on operators slide a fresh tire into place, ready for the nut to be tightened.

WHEEL GUN

Tire gunners use this tool to loosen and tighten wheel nuts. Powered by compressed air, wheel guns rotate over 10,000 times per minute!

FRONT JACK

The front jack operator slides the jack under the front wing, lifts the car, then shifts to the side so they're ready to lower the car and remove the jack.

THE GARAGE

Lined against the pit wall are all the teams' garages, staffed with expert mechanics, engineers, and specialists. They're high-tech and busy places: engines rev, wheel guns whine, and screens scroll with endless data . . .

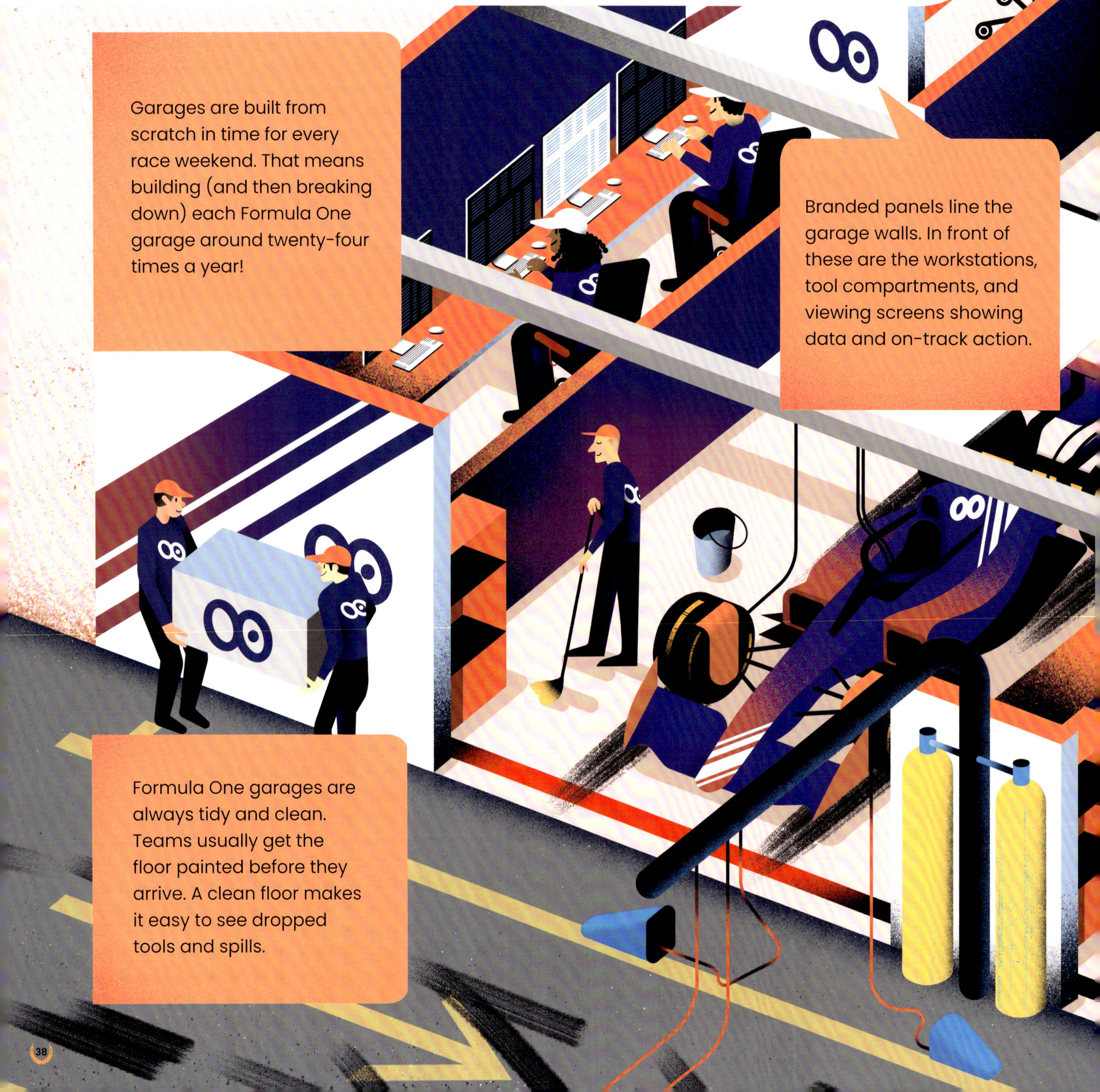

Garages are built from scratch in time for every race weekend. That means building (and then breaking down) each Formula One garage around twenty-four times a year!

Branded panels line the garage walls. In front of these are the workstations, tool compartments, and viewing screens showing data and on-track action.

Formula One garages are always tidy and clean. Teams usually get the floor painted before they arrive. A clean floor makes it easy to see dropped tools and spills.

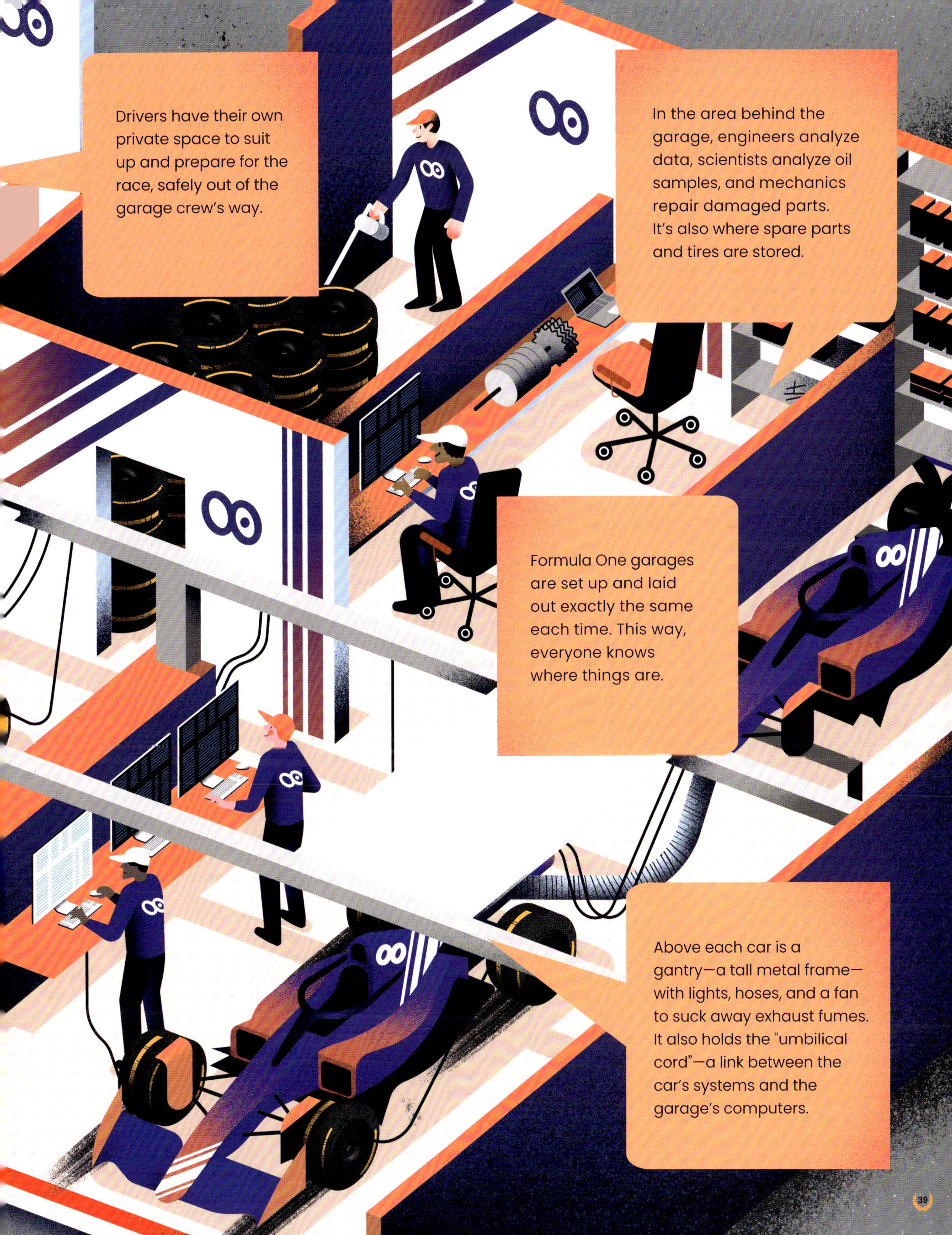
Drivers have their own private space to suit up and prepare for the race, safely out of the garage crew's way.
In the area behind the garage, engineers analyze data, scientists analyze oil samples, and mechanics repair damaged parts. It's also where spare parts and tires are stored.
Formula One garages are set up and laid out exactly the same each time. This way, everyone knows where things are.
Above each car is a gantry—a tall metal frame—with lights, hoses, and a fan to suck away exhaust fumes. It also holds the "umbilical cord"—a link between the car's systems and the garage's computers.

LEGENDARY CIRCUITS

Grand Prix have been hosted on nearly eighty racetrack circuits around the world—on every continent except Antarctica! Every circuit is different, with their own "feel" and quirks. Some rise above all others to become legends.

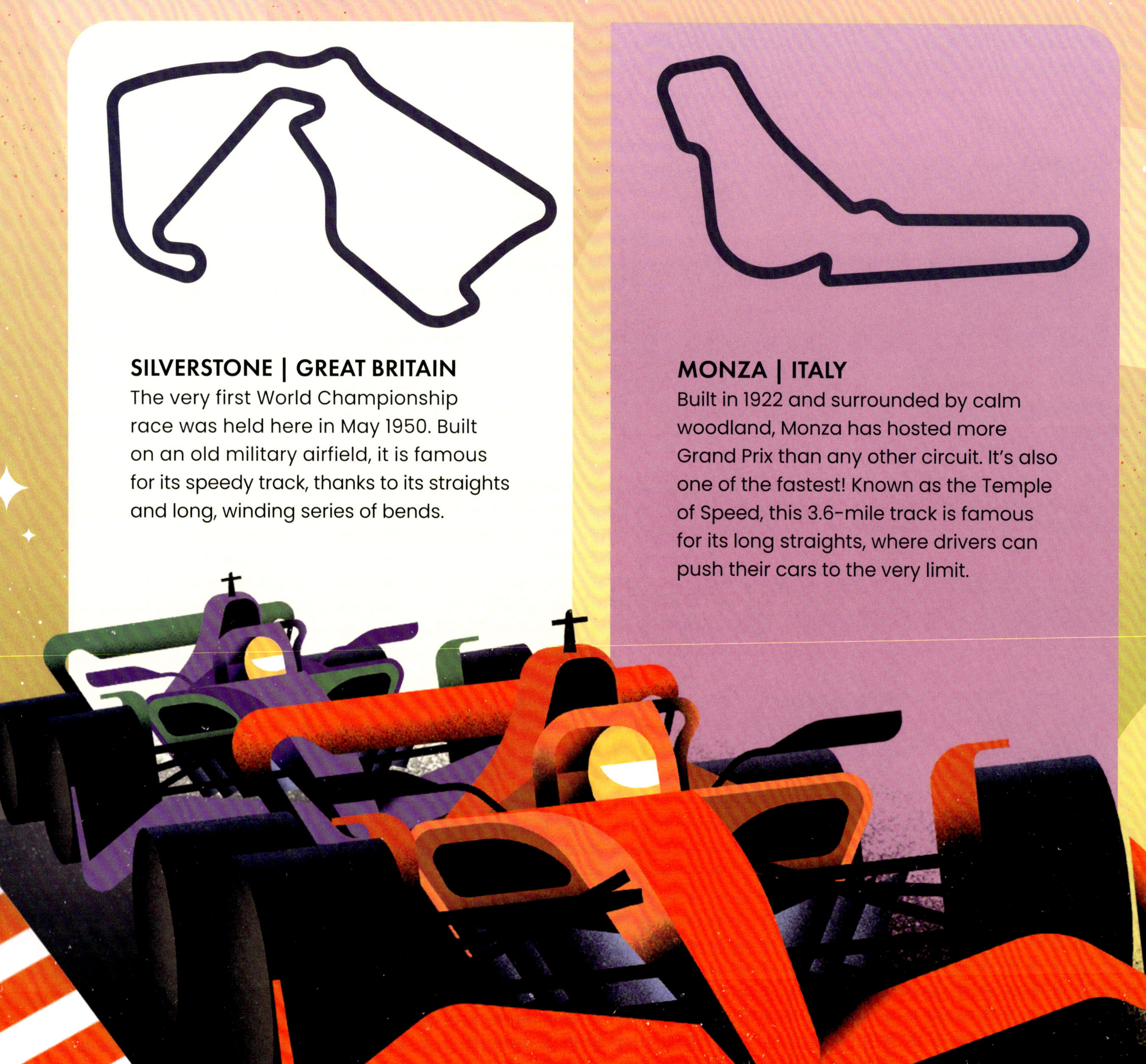

SILVERSTONE | GREAT BRITAIN
The very first World Championship race was held here in May 1950. Built on an old military airfield, it is famous for its speedy track, thanks to its straights and long, winding series of bends.

MONZA | ITALY
Built in 1922 and surrounded by calm woodland, Monza has hosted more Grand Prix than any other circuit. It's also one of the fastest! Known as the Temple of Speed, this 3.6-mile track is famous for its long straights, where drivers can push their cars to the very limit.

SPA-FRANCORCHAMPS | BELGIUM

One of the most beautiful circuits in the world, Spa-Francorchamps is a highlight of the racing season. Opened in 1921, the original track included public roads and was 9.3 miles long. The modern circuit is only half that length. With its steep slopes and fast corners, it's a tricky one to master.

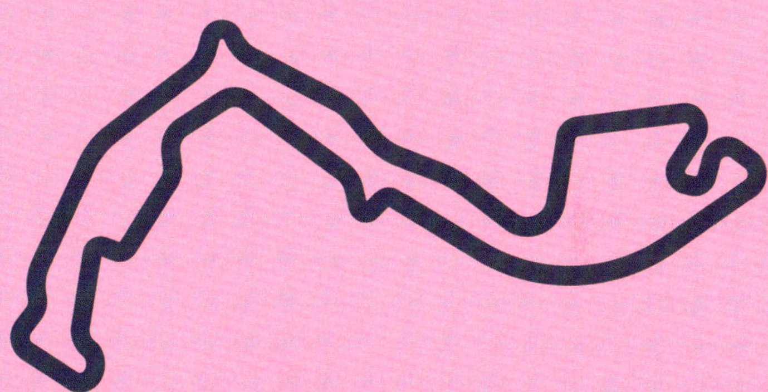

MONACO | MONACO

Perhaps the most famous Grand Prix circuit. Since 1929, the race has been held on the streets of this tiny Mediterranean city-state. Its tight corners, narrow track sections, and a dark tunnel make overtaking extremely difficult. Because of its challenging layout, the Monaco Grand Prix is 28 miles shorter than most others.

LAS VEGAS | UNITED STATES

Las Vegas saw its first Formula One race in 2023. It is a temporary street circuit, meaning it uses some of the city's regular roads as part of the racetrack. Cars even speed along part of the famous Las Vegas Strip. The fact that it's held at night, showing off the city's eye-popping neon lights, makes it truly unique.

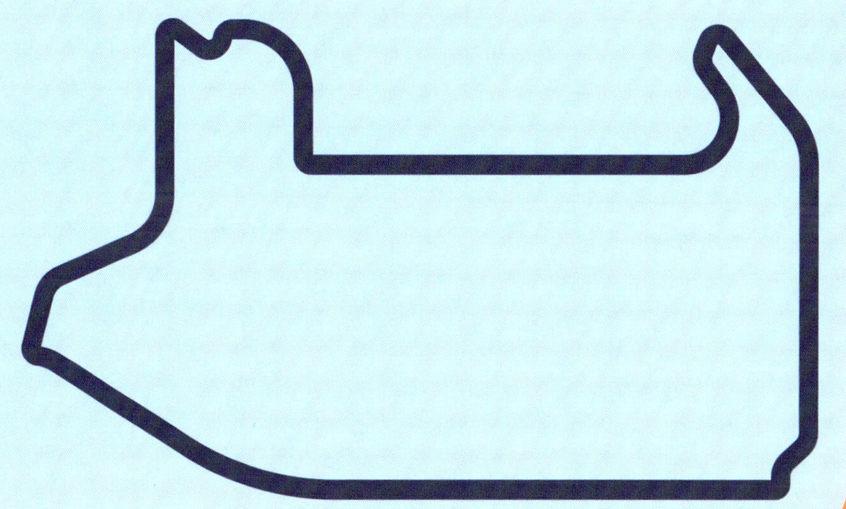

TRAIN TO WIN

Imagine sitting in the cockpit—the engine is roaring and you are zooming along at 200 mph, enduring G-forces similar to those experienced by fighter pilots.

How can you train to win in these tough conditions?

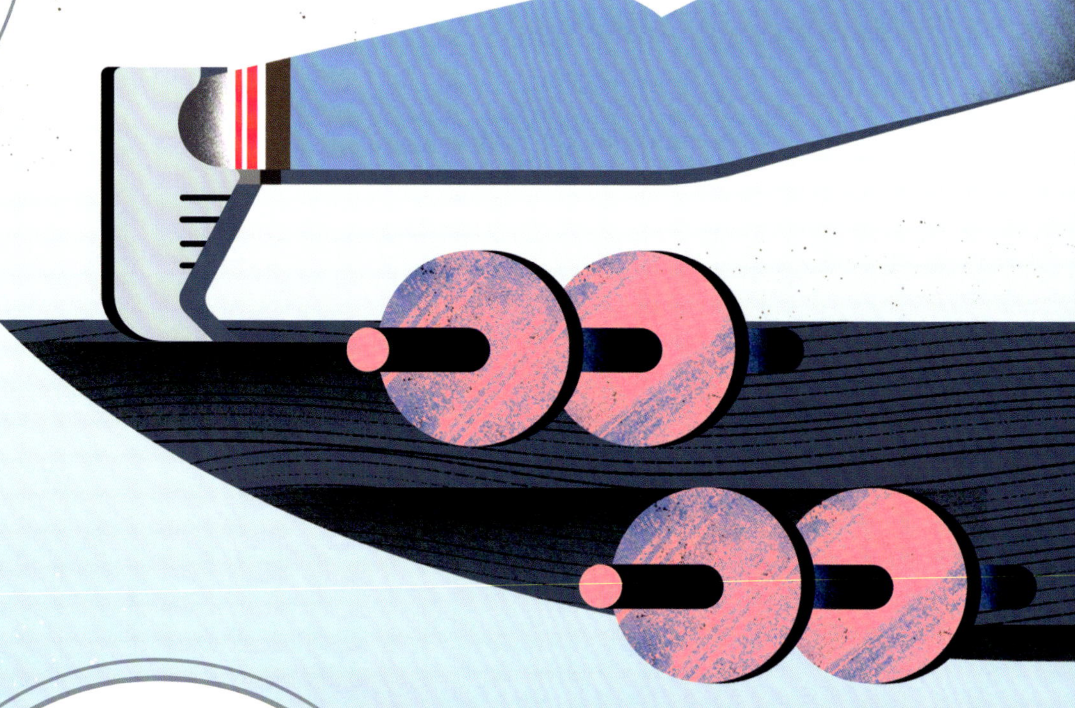

PHYSICAL TRAINING

Drivers lift weights to build strength—sturdy neck muscles are essential to handle the strong G-forces when racing. Races are long and tough, so drivers improve their fitness by running, cycling, and swimming. They also need to be quick and flexible (to get out of a crashed car, for example), so they'll do yoga and stretching.

REFLEX TRAINING

When racing, drivers need fast reflexes to react quickly. The smallest mistake can mean the loss of a position or even cause an accident. Before a race, drivers perform exercises such as catching balls to improve their reflexes and hand-eye coordination.

DIET

Every meal is planned to give all the nutrition and energy the driver needs. They eat lots of nuts, vegetables, fruit, berries, lean meat, fish, pulses like beans and lentils, and drink protein shakes. Drivers are rarely seen without a bottle of water—they can lose 4–6 lb in sweat during a race!

BRAIN TRAINING

Competing in a high-level and dangerous sport requires mental strength, self-confidence, and the ability to stay calm. Some drivers work with specialists to help them practice mindfulness, which involves being more "in the moment" and helps with worries. This can also help them bounce back after bad race results.

REST AND RECOVERY

Rest is as important as work. After a race or training session, drivers often have cold baths and massages to help with sore muscles, followed by a good night's sleep so they're ready for the next day's challenges.

THE ROAD TO FORMULA ONE

Although only twenty-two drivers race in Formula One, there are plenty of up-and-coming athletes fighting for their chance to compete at the top.

Would you have what it takes?

KARTING

Most Formula One drivers start their careers racing karts when they are as young as eight years old—sometimes even younger!

Driving zippy karts lets young drivers find out what it's like to drive competitively—but without the danger of real cars.

FORMULA FOUR

Talented fifteen-year-old kart drivers can start competing in Formula Four championships around the world.

They compete in cars that look like Formula One cars—but are far less powerful, high-tech, and expensive.

FORMULA THREE

When they are sixteen or older, young drivers may be accepted to compete in a Formula Three championship.

By driving more powerful cars in front of larger crowds, drivers get a taste of what it's like to be in the top levels of the sport. Success here will be noticed.

FORMULA TWO

Formula Two is the final stepping stone to Formula One. To compete, drivers must be seventeen.

Formula Two cars are identical. They can hit 200 mph, reaching 60 mph in 2.8 seconds! This means the only difference between the drivers is skill.

LIFE IN THE FAST LANE

Formula One drivers are expected to do a lot more than just race. During the racing season, they might be preparing for the next race, doing interviews, or meeting fans. Here are some of the things they get up to.

KNOWLEDGE IS POWER

Every race weekend, lots of technical information and data is shared between the drivers, engineers, and technicians in meeting after meeting after meeting. They also talk about their successes and failures and discuss rule changes.

NEWSWORTHY

Lots of news outlets want to cover the on-track action, as well as the behind-the-scenes dealmaking and gossip. And they all want to talk to the drivers. To help, drivers are given media training. They prepare what to say and, just as important, what *not* to say. After all, teams don't want to give away their secrets!

FAN SERVICE

Formula One is famous for having enthusiastic fans—and they often want to meet the drivers. Drivers do a lot of work to keep fans happy. Sometimes they chat with fans, sign autographs, and take selfies. Or, they answer questions in front of cheering crowds—even during busy race weekends.

KEEPING THE SPONSORS HAPPY

It's incredibly expensive to run a Formula One team. To help pay for this, teams look for sponsors—companies that give them money in return for advertising, such as having their company logo on the car.

Sometimes sponsors want to get close to the drivers too. So fancy events are put on with the driver as a special guest, to keep the sponsors happy.

LUXURY LIFESTYLE

Formula One drivers work very hard for their success. Their hard work does not go unrewarded! Drivers travel the world in style, staying in five-star hotels, and are paid extremely well. They are sometimes even given or loaned luxury sports cars.

FORMULA FEMALE

Since it began, most of the people working in Formula One have been men, from engineers to drivers. Only five women have raced in Formula One so far! This is despite people of all genders having the same potential to do any job in motorsport. But things are starting to change . . .

FAST CARS, SLOW PROGRESS

When Formula One began, attitudes toward women were very different from today. Motorsport was seen as too dangerous for women.

Now, 40 percent of Formula One fans are female. There are some incredible women in the sport, such as Monisha Kaltenborn, the first female team principal. But Formula One still needs a lot more female role models to inspire girls to get into motorsport.

POSITIVE STEPS

In 2023, an all-female annual F1 Academy racing series began. It was started to create opportunities for women in motorsport and to inspire girls and young women.

The goal is to help skilled female drivers progress to higher levels of racing so that everyone has the chance to compete at the very top. Plus, live TV coverage of their races means even more action for fans to watch!

F1 ACADEMY CHAMPIONSHIP

Fifteen female drivers representing five teams compete in the F1 Academy championship. There are fourteen races per season. The drivers sit behind the wheel of identical Formula 4 racing cars, boasting a top speed of 149 mph.

Stars are already shining bright in F1 Academy, including Chloe Chambers (United States), Aurelia Nobels (Brazil), and winner of the very first championship, Marta García (Spain).

ICONIC DRIVERS

In the center of the storm—among the cheering fans and busy mechanics—are the drivers. Strapped in, eyes fixed ahead, they all want to win fame and glory. Many race, but few become legends.

JUAN MANUEL FANGIO (ACTIVE 1950–1958)

RACE WINS: 24 | F1 CHAMPIONSHIP WINS: 5

Argentinian Juan Manuel Fangio dominated Formula One's first decade. His five championship victories were made with four different teams—an unbroken record. He is also the oldest champion ever, winning his fifth title at forty-six.

MARIA TERESA DE FILIPPIS (ACTIVE 1958–1959)

F1 RACE ENTRIES: 5 | BEST FINISH: 10TH

Italian driver Maria Teresa de Filippis was the first female driver to compete in a Formula One Championship. Despite driving an "old" Maserati 250F, she entered five Grand Prix and came in 10th place in the 1958 Belgian Grand Prix.

JIM CLARK (ACTIVE 1960–1968)

RACE WINS: 25 | F1 CHAMPIONSHIP WINS: 2

Scottish-born Jim Clark won many Grand Prix races in the 1960s—arguably motorsport's most dangerous decade. Clark even won the 1967 Dutch Grand Prix in the legendary Lotus 49, despite never having driven the car before that race weekend!

NIKI LAUDA (ACTIVE 1971–1979 AND 1982–1985)

RACE WINS: 25 | F1 CHAMPIONSHIP WINS: 3

Few Formula One drivers have shown more grit than Austrian legend Niki Lauda. In 1976, he crashed his Ferrari 312T. After surviving severe injuries, he was back racing six weeks later—and came second in the championship.

DESIRÉ WILSON (ACTIVE 1980)

BRITISH F1 CHAMPIONSHIP WINS: 1

South African Desiré Wilson earned a place in the 1980 Formula One World Championship, although she failed to qualify. However, she did win a Grand Prix at Brands Hatch during the short-lived British Formula One Championship. She is (so far) the only woman to win a Formula One race.

AYRTON SENNA (ACTIVE 1984–1994)

RACE WINS: 41 | F1 CHAMPIONSHIP WINS: 3

With a long-standing—now broken—record of sixty-five **pole positions** (first starting positions), Brazilian legend Ayrton Senna was famous for his off-track charm. In the 1993 European Grand Prix, he jumped from fifth to first place in a stunning upset that fans called the "Lap of the Gods."

MICHAEL SCHUMACHER (ACTIVE 1991–2006 AND 2010–2012)

RACE WINS: 91 | F1 CHAMPIONSHIP WINS: 7

German driver Michael Schumacher won seven championships, 91 Grand Prix victories, and 68 pole positions. Nicknamed "the Rainmaster," he had incredible skill racing in wet weather. His amazing fitness regimen is now standard practice in Formula One.

LEWIS HAMILTON (ACTIVE 2007–PRESENT)

(AT START OF 2025) RACE WINS: 105 | F1 CHAMPIONSHIP WINS: 7

In 2020, British driver Lewis Hamilton equaled Schumacher with seven championship wins. As of the 2024 season, his records include the most Grand Prix victories, pole positions, and podium finishes (over 200!), mostly while driving for the Mercedes team.

MAX VERSTAPPEN (ACTIVE 2015–PRESENT)

(AT START OF 2025) RACE WINS: 63 | F1 CHAMPIONSHIP WINS: 4

Dutch speedster Max Verstappen has a stunning victory rate: in the 2023 season, he won over 86 percent of the races! He is also the youngest driver to ever take part in a World Championship race, at only 17 years and 166 days old.

DRIVERS MAKING A DIFFERENCE

Formula One holds races all over the world and attracts fans from every continent. And yet most of the people involved in the sport since it began—from engineers and team principals to mechanics and drivers—are white. Now some people are trying to change this.

LEWIS'S MISSION

In the United Kingdom—home to seven of the eleven Formula One teams—fewer than 1 percent of people in motorsport are Black. As the first (and so far only) Black driver in the history of Formula One, Lewis Hamilton is passionate about changing this.

THE HAMILTON COMMISSION

With the help of the Royal Academy of Engineering, Hamilton set up a report called The Hamilton Commission. Its aim is to find the problems preventing Black people from entering motorsport, and make a plan for change.

The report came out in 2021. It has three main suggestions:

1. SUPPORT AND EMPOWERMENT

Make it easier for young Black people to work and progress in STEM (Science, Technology, Engineering, and Math) jobs.

For example, the report suggests that Formula One teams should hire more apprentices (people who learn a trade on a job rather than going to college), and help people who can't afford to work in motorsport.

2. ACCOUNTABILITY AND MEASUREMENT

Ask people in important positions, such as team owners and managers, to make sure their teams are diverse (have lots of different types of people in them).

For example, they could collect and share data on the people in their teams, and make sure everyone is valued and respected.

3. INSPIRATION AND ENGAGEMENT

Inspire young Black people with role models in Formula One and show them what working in motorsport is like.

For example, the report suggests creating lessons for students to learn about Black scientists and the amazing work they do.

THE TEAM WORKS

Drivers may be the superstars, but there are many incredible people on a modern racing team. Here are some of the different jobs they do.

Which job would you choose?

TEAM PRINCIPAL

This is the head of the team. They are in charge of all departments and make all major decisions. They also speak for the team publicly in interviews.

This is a tricky job: you need to be good at communicating, have technical know-how, and keep track of the ever-changing rules. It's stressful too—if the team does badly, the team principal is blamed!

TECHNICAL DIRECTOR

Designing and building a Formula One car involves many special departments and hundreds of engineers. The technical director is responsible for the car's design and in charge of all the technical teams.

TECHNICAL DEPARTMENT HEADS

Formula One cars are incredibly complicated, so it would be impossible for one person to know everything about how to make a great car. That's why each team has specialist departments (such as power unit, driver communication, and safety), which are headed by people who are experts in each area.

HEAD OF COMMUNICATIONS

The communications department makes sure the public has a good opinion of the team. They do everything from organizing photo and video shoots to teaching drivers how to give interviews. Sometimes they even help design the car's color scheme (the "livery.")

RESERVE DRIVERS

Often up-and-coming racers, reserve drivers are substitutes who compete if a main driver gets sick or injured. Do well, and they might become a main driver themselves! They're also used as test drivers to try out new car features.

COMMERCIAL DIRECTOR

Formula One teams need money. Without it, they can't develop cars, pay staff, or travel to races. Commercial directors look after this money. They also have to keep their sponsors happy season after season, and find new sponsors.

FAMOUS TEAMS

Around 170 constructors (teams) have aimed to win Formula One glory. Many make brave but short attempts before being forgotten. Some compete hard for decades and write their names into racing history. A few become Formula One legends.

COOPER CAR COMPANY (JOHN & CHARLES COOPER)

Working from their small garage in England, father and son Charles and John Cooper revolutionized Formula One. In the late 1950s, when front-engine cars were all the rage, their rear-engine wonder-car beat the racing giants of the day. Everyone soon copied the Coopers' design.

BRABHAM (JACK BRABHAM & RON TAURANAC)

Founded in 1960 by Australian racer Jack Brabham and British-Australian engineer Ron Tauranac, Brabham became the largest manufacturer of racing cars in the world. Jack Brabham won the Drivers' Championship twice for Cooper and then once for Brabham—he is the only driver to win it in a car bearing his own name.

LOTUS (COLIN CHAPMAN)
Founded in England by car designer Colin Chapman in 1952, Lotus invented many incredible technologies that transformed Formula One. They were the first to use the monocoque chassis (in the Lotus 25), the stressed-member engine (Lotus 49), and the "ground effect" car (Lotus 78).

WILLIAMS (FRANK WILLIAMS)
British-born Frank Williams had a tricky start with his racing team, but in 1979 they won their first Grand Prix. Despite being involved in a life-changing car accident in 1986, Williams continued his success and his team won nine Constructors' and seven Drivers' Championships.

MCLAREN (BRUCE MCLAREN)
New Zealand racing car driver, designer, and engineer Bruce McLaren achieved a lot in the thirty-two years before his tragic death in 1970 while testing a racing car. McLaren, the racing team he founded in 1963, is his legacy. Driven by greats such as Ayrton Senna and Niki Lauda, McLaren has won twelve Drivers' Championships and eight Constructors' Championships.

FERRARI (ENZO FERRARI)
Everyone knows the name Ferrari and their bright red cars. Founded in 1929 in Italy by retired driver Enzo Ferrari, Ferrari went on to become the most long-lasting and successful Formula One team in history. They have more Grand Prix wins, pole positions, and fastest laps than any other team!

MONEY TALKS

As the world's top motorsport, Formula One is famous for its glitz and glamour. It's no surprise to learn it makes an awful lot of money—more than $3.6 billion a year!

COST CAP

Running a Formula One team is expensive, and some teams have more money than others. So, to make things fairer (and make the sport more competitive and exciting), there is a "cost cap"—a limit on the amount of money a team is allowed to spend every season. Before the cap, some teams were spending over $400 million a season!

WINNER GETS THE SPOILS

As with most sports, there's prize money up for grabs—and lots of it. Prize money is paid by the FIA to the teams, with the season champion getting the biggest cut, and so on down to last place.

The winner also gets a trophy—but they are kept by the teams. The driver often has to buy a replica!

DRIVE TO SURVIVE

Drivers don't receive prize money from the FIA. Instead, they get paid by their team. Top drivers earn tens of millions per season: Dutch driver Max Verstappen was paid over $65 million in 2025! Most drivers will also get a winner's bonus from their team for a good finishing position.

CASHING IN

Because Formula One has a huge global audience, big brands are happy to pay money to sponsor it. And the more successful a Formula One team is, the more cash they can get from sponsors.

Teams can also make money by selling merchandise, such as clothing with their team logo on it.

CAPTURING AN AUDIENCE

Grand Prix are held all over the world. This means spectators can watch races at their local circuit. Over 6.5 million fans attended races in the 2024 season!

Millions more watch Formula One on TV, tuning in to watch interviews, hear expert analysis, and see all the on-track action. Companies pay lots of money to advertise their products during these broadcasts.

PODIUM FINISH

Now we've reached the finish line!

We've met some of the most famous drivers, visited the most iconic circuits, and sat in some of the most historic cars.

We've witnessed pit crews perform lightning-fast tire changes, followed drivers as they strive to be the best, and visited the many departments that keep a Formula One team racing.

We've seen how Formula One is starting to change for the better, putting female drivers in the spotlight and welcoming people from different backgrounds.

And you can be a part of Formula One too! You could work in a team factory, be part of a pit crew, or even line up on the grid in your own car. Whether you end up racing or you simply enjoy the action as a fan, Formula One can be a thrilling and inspiring part of your life.

The future is fast!

GLOSSARY

ACTIVE SUSPENSION
Computer-controlled suspension that helps keep a vehicle stable when moving.

ANTI-LOCK BRAKES
An anti-lock braking system (ABS) is an automatic system that helps drivers avoid skidding and "locking up" the brakes.

BIOMETRIC
Measurements of biology (the workings of a person's body), including heart rate and blood pressure.

BREATHABLE
A fabric that allows air to pass through it. Helps to keep the wearer cool and dry.

CHASSIS
The stiff, strong frame of the car that the main components (wheels, engine, seats, etc.) are fixed to.

CLUTCH
Mechanical device that disconnects the gearbox (transmission) from the engine to allow the driver to shift gears. In modern Formula One cars, the driver only uses the clutch to stop and start the car, not shift gears.

COCKPIT
Where the driver sits in the car.

CONSTRUCTORS
Formula One racing teams who design and build cars. Each team races two cars in each Grand Prix.

CONSTRUCTORS' CHAMPIONSHIP
The Formula One competition won by the racing team that has won the most points over a season.

CORNERING
Driving around a corner (a bend in the racetrack).

DATA
Information, particularly facts or numbers, that is collected and analyzed to make decisions.

DOWNFORCE
A downward-pushing force created by air flowing over a moving vehicle. Formula One cars are designed to increase downforce to improve the car's stability.

DRAG
A force that slows the car down, making it harder to move.

DRIVERS' CHAMPIONSHIP
The Formula One competition won by the individual driver who has won the most points over a season.

ENERGY RECOVERY SYSTEM (ERS)
Part of a hybrid power unit (engine) that gathers energy from the heat generated by the ICE (internal combustion engine) and from actions such as braking. The energy is stored in batteries. Drivers can use that stored energy to give their car a speed boost.

FIA
Fédération Internationale de l'Automobile. The governing body that oversees all aspects of Formula One.

FOUR-WHEEL DRIVE
A system that provides power to all four wheels of a vehicle.

G-FORCE
Gravity-force. A unit that measures the rate of acceleration (speeding up) and deceleration (slowing down).

GAS TURBINE
A powerful engine that uses a flow of gas to rotate blades in a turbine (similar to a rotating propellor on an airplane), creating energy.

GRAND PRIX
A race in Formula One; this is the main event of a race weekend.

GRID POSITION
A driver's position on the starting grid at the beginning of a race.

GRIP
Friction between the tires and the track.

GROUND EFFECT
When the underside of a racing car is designed to affect the air below the body, causing the car to "stick" to the track. This improves cornering.

HANDLING
How well the car can be controlled, especially when steering and braking at high speeds.

INDICATOR LIGHT
Red light at the rear of the car. Used to help drivers see the car ahead during poor visibility conditions, such as rain.

INTERNAL COMBUSTION ENGINE (ICE)
An engine that generates power by burning fuel, such as gas, with air. The power created is converted into movement.

LAP
One complete circuit (loop) of a track.

LAPPED
When a car is overtaken (passed) by a car that is already one lap ahead.

MANUAL GEARBOX
A gearbox that needs a driver's input (pushing a button or a switch, or pressing a clutch and moving a "stick") to shift gears up and down according to how fast the car is going.

MONOCOQUE
A type of chassis in racing cars, where the car's outer body, or frame, bears the weight of all the components, such as the wheels and the engine. This makes the vehicle stronger, lighter, and more fuel efficient.

OVERTAKE
To pass another car on the track.

PIT STOP
A short break during a race where the car enters the pit box for tire changes and repairs. This process is sometimes called "pitting."

POLE POSITION
The first starting position on the track. The driver with the best qualifying time gets to start here.

QUALIFYING
The sessions (mini races) in the lead-up to a Grand Prix. These rounds decide who appears on the starting grid, including who is in pole position.

RADIATOR
Part of an engine's cooling system.

SEMIAUTOMATIC GEARBOX
Drivers manually shift the gears up and down, but without having to use a clutch.

TITANIUM
A strong, lightweight metal used in many things, including medical equipment, computers, spacecraft, and airplanes.

TRACTION CONTROL
An electronic system that can tell if a car is losing grip—it automatically applies the brakes to regain control.

TURBOCHARGED ENGINE
An engine that directs the car's exhaust gases through a turbine to increase its power.

ABOUT THE AUTHOR AND ILLUSTRATOR

Matt Ralphs is an author and editor. His children's nonfiction books include *Spooky Celebrations Around the World*, *Beasts from the Deep*, *Transported*, *Automotive,* and *Around the World in 80 Inventions*. He has lots of interests, especially Formula One and fast cars in general, and counts himself lucky that he gets to write books about them.

Dragan Kordić is a Croatian illustrator and designer. His work ranges from illustrations for publishing and public spaces to visuals for startups, corporate clients, and advertising. He is inspired by nature, travel, and books. He lives in Rijeka, Croatia, with his wife and daughter.